# A to Z Coloring Book on Fun Facts About Nature

Written by Margie LeRoux

Illustrated by Sharon Wood

Copyright © 2018 Margie LeRoux

All rights reserved.

ISBN-10: 1726299511

ISBN-13: 978-1726299510

# Content

A is for Antelope — 1
B is for Beaver — 2
C is for Cow — 3
D is for Deer — 4
E is for Eel — 5
F is for Frog — 6
G is for Goat — 7
H is for Heron — 8
I is for Iguana — 9
J is for Jellyfish — 10
K is for Koala — 11
L is for Llama — 12
M is for Mouse — 13
N is for Nightingale — 14
O is for Ostrich — 15
P is for Pig — 16
Q is for Quail — 17
R is for Raccoon — 18
S is for Sheep — 19
T is for Turtle — 20
U is for Umbrellabird — 21
V is for Vulture — 22
W is for Walrus — 23
X is for X-Ray Tetra — 24
Y is for Yak — 25
Z is for Zebra — 26

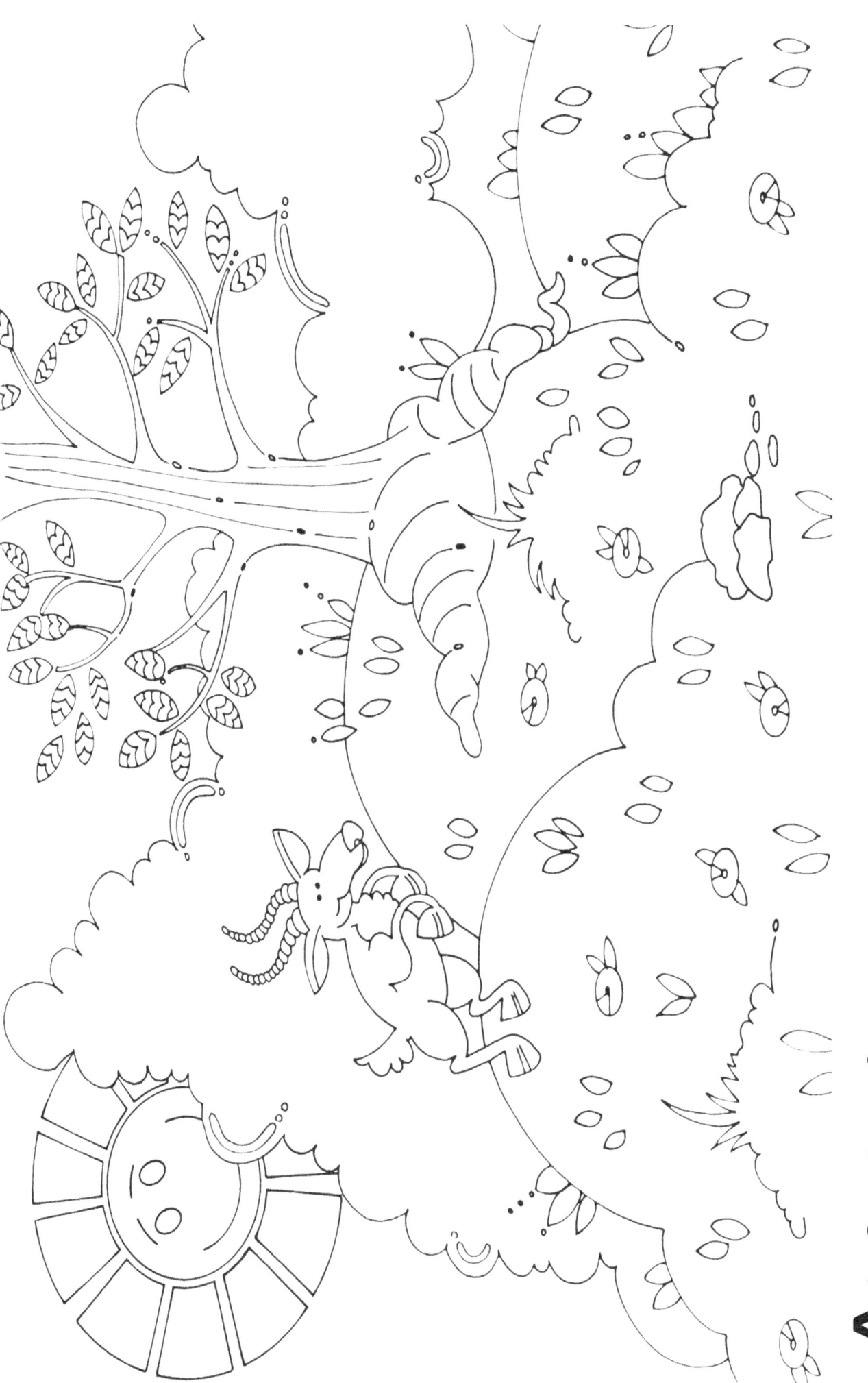

# A is for Antelope
– Antelope are smart. They follow the rain to find tender grass to eat.

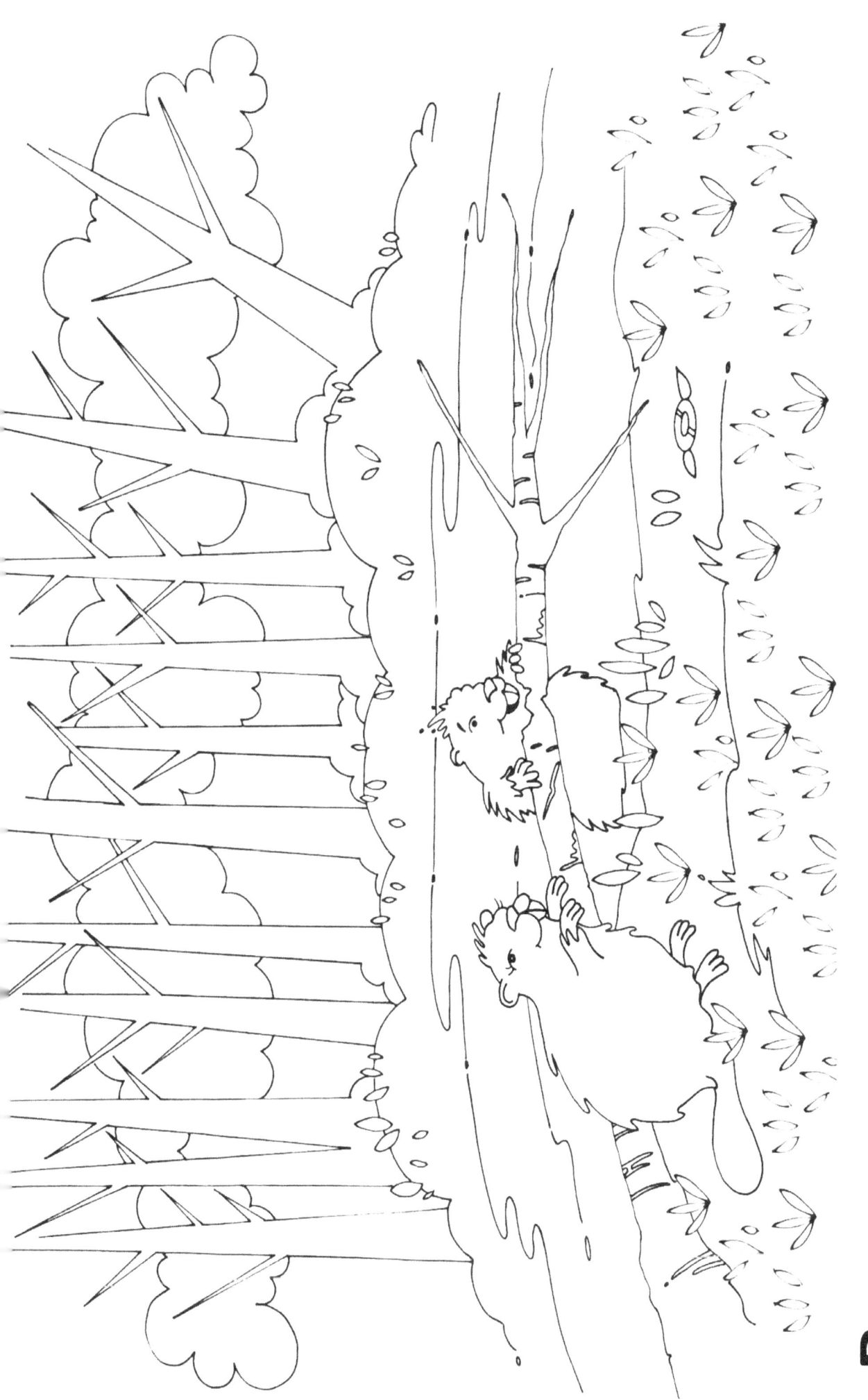

**B is for Beaver** – Beavers teeth never stop growing so they gnaw on wood to keep them from getting too long.

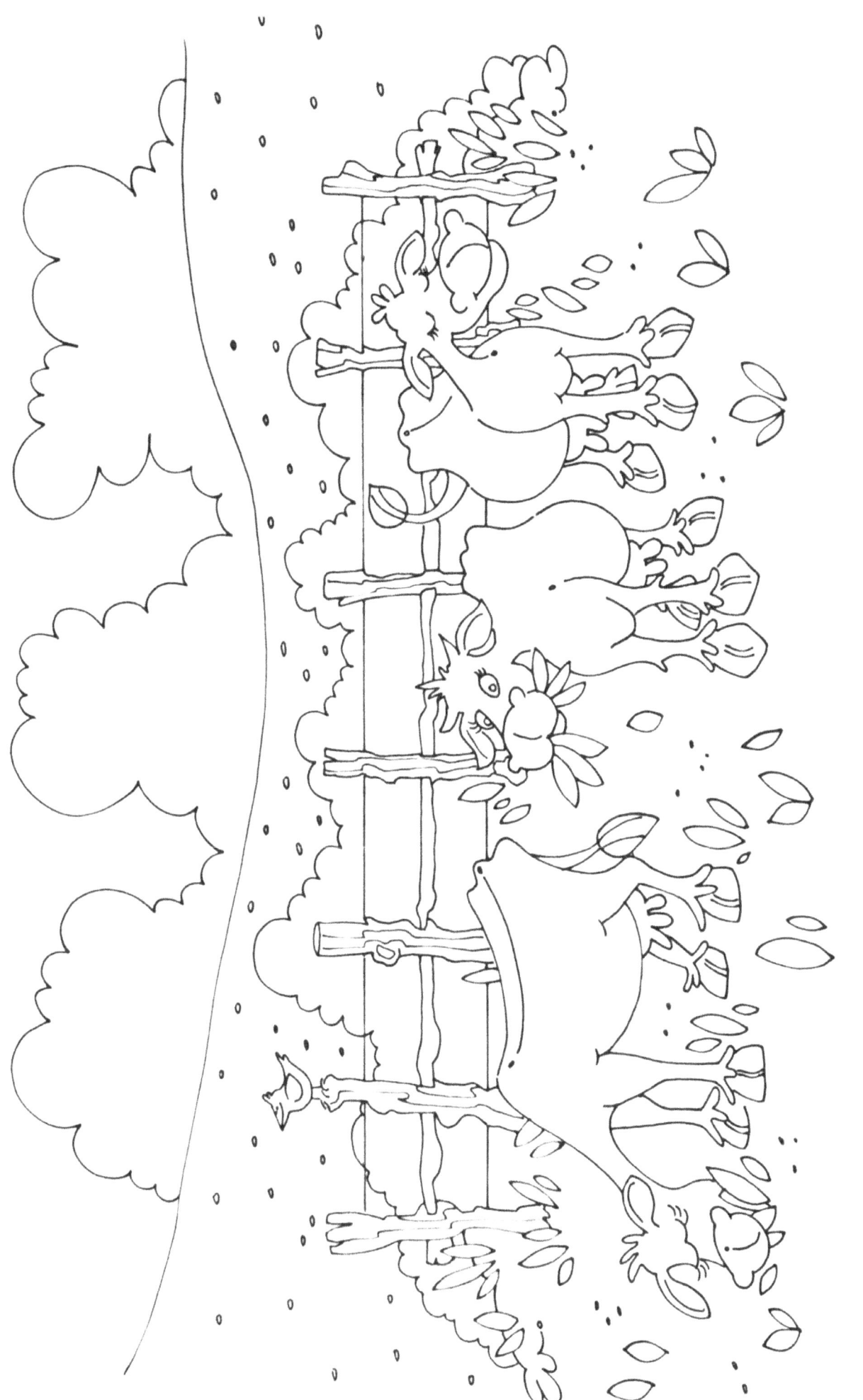

# C is for Cow — Cows eat 8 hours a day and can sleep standing up.

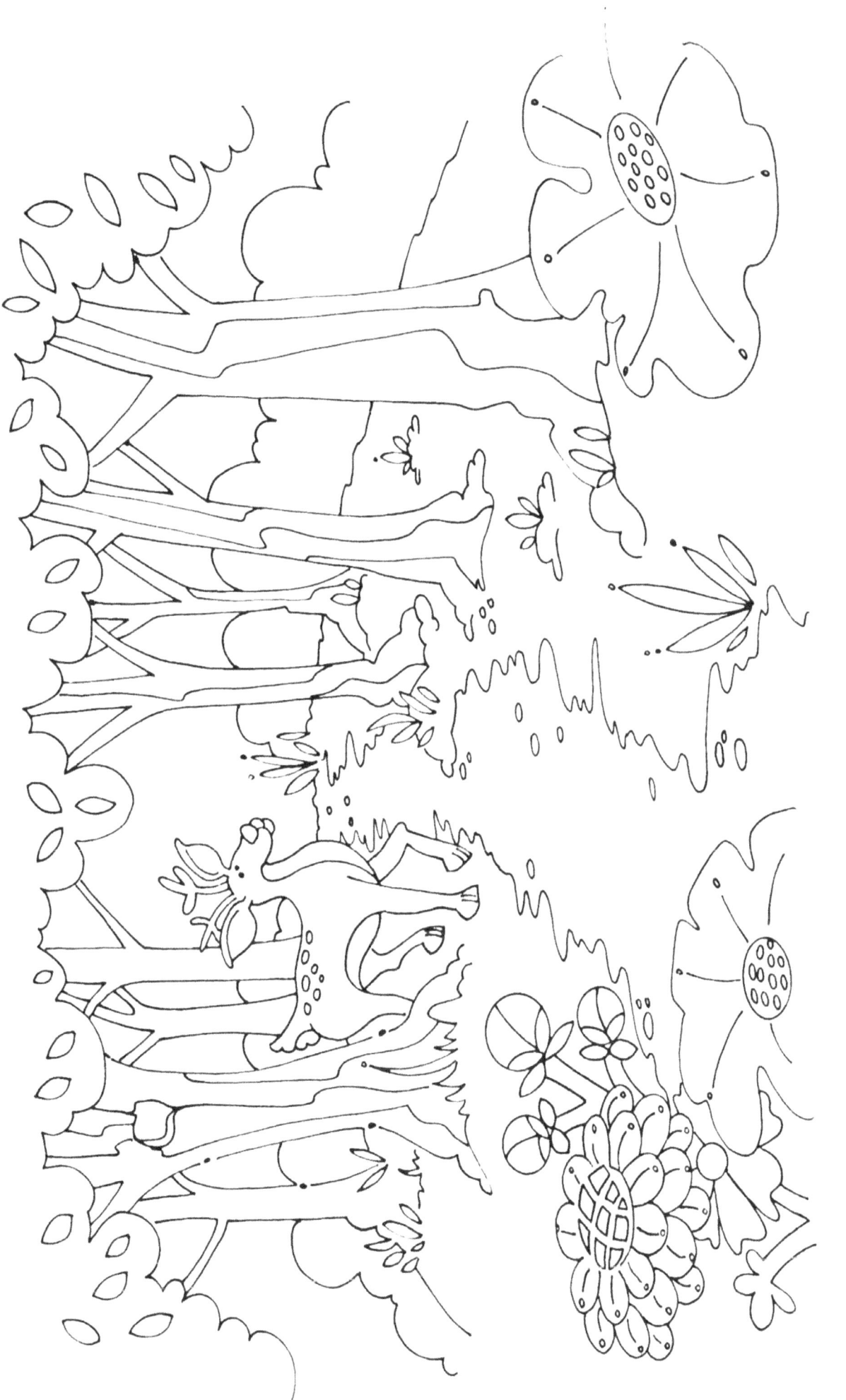

# D is for Deer – A male Deer is called a Buck and grows new antlers every year.

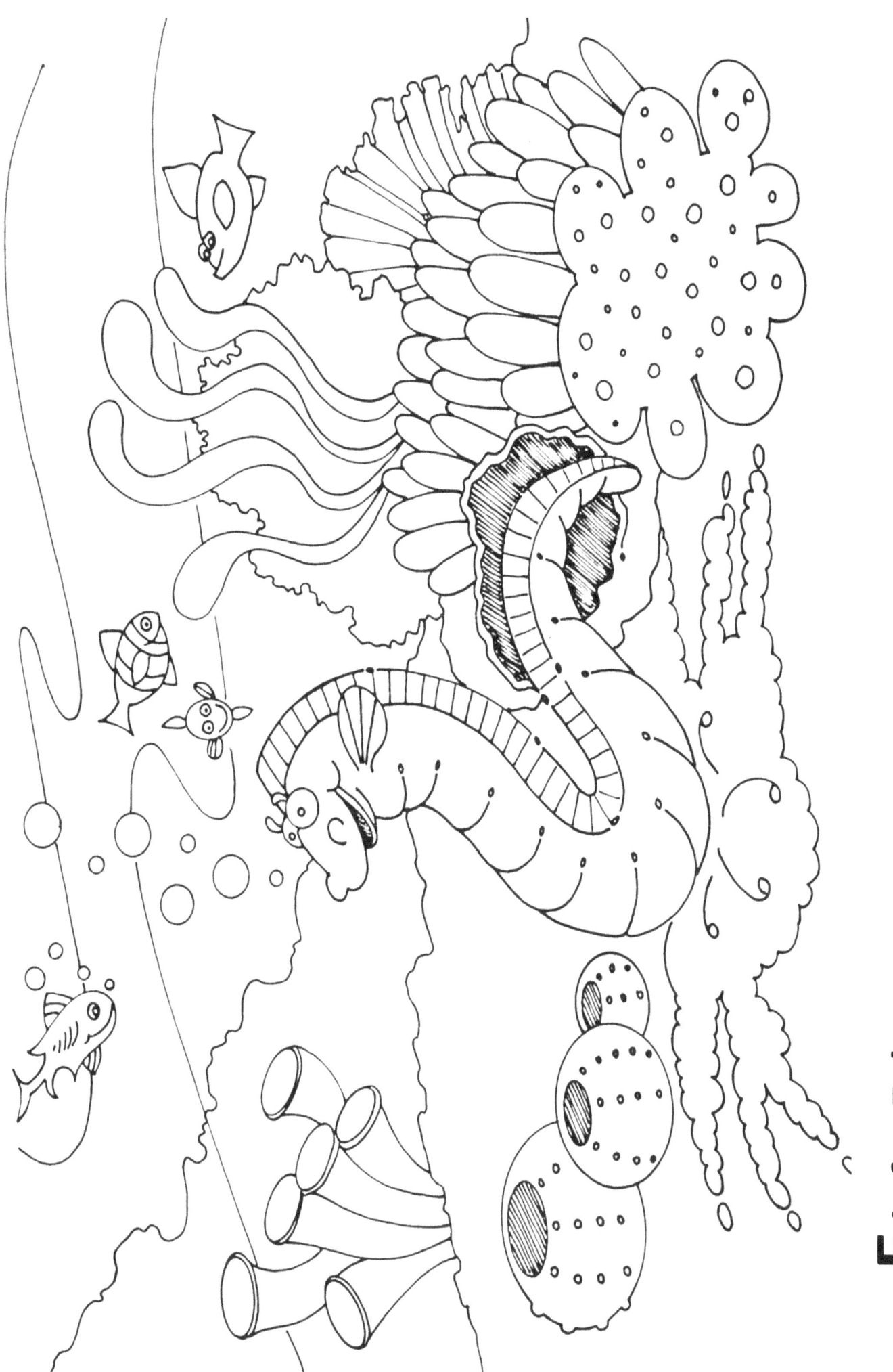

**E is for Eel** – Eels live in the ocean and can swim forwards and backwards.

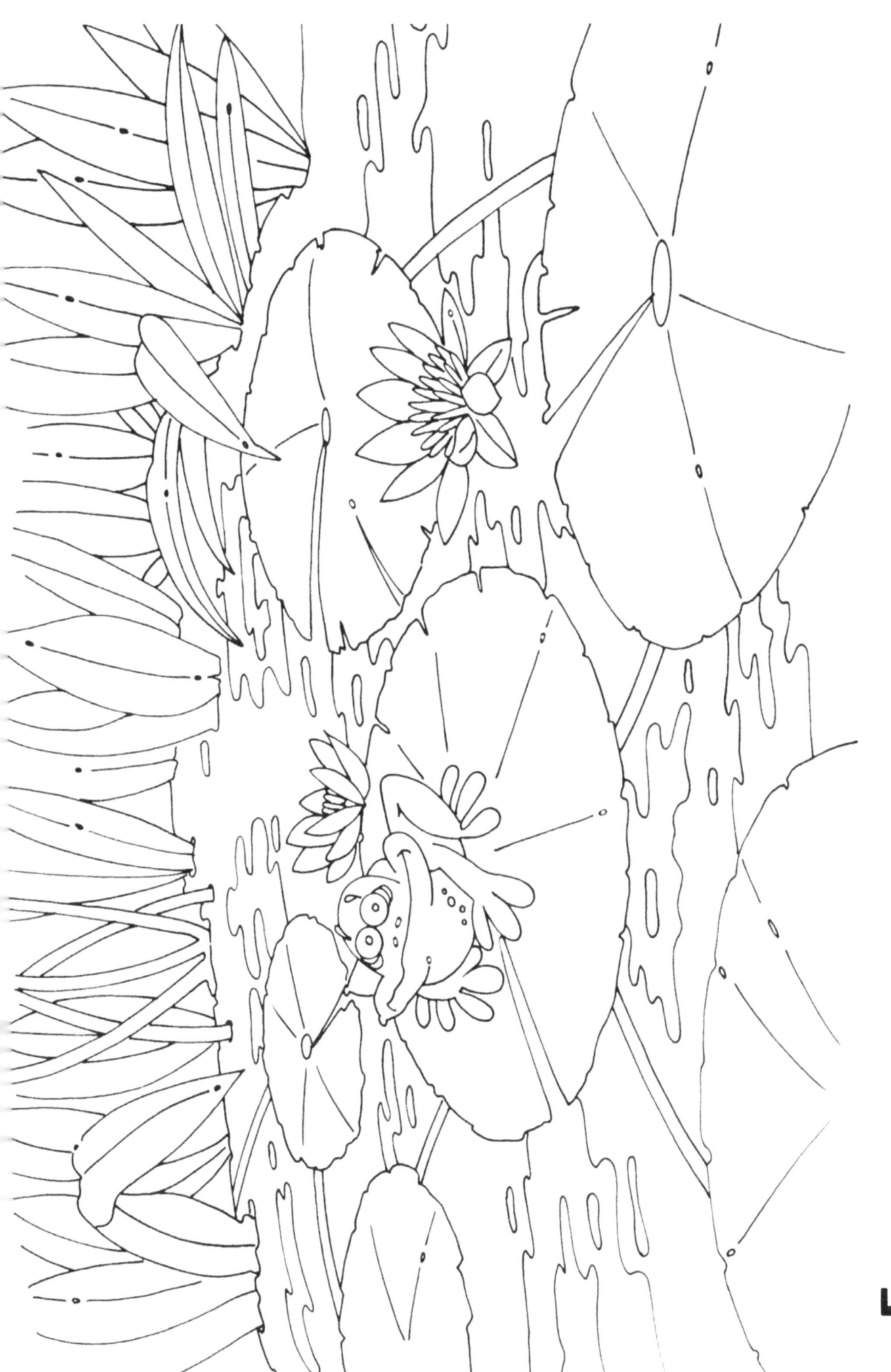

**F is for Frog** — Frogs can see forwards, sideways, and upwards at the same time.

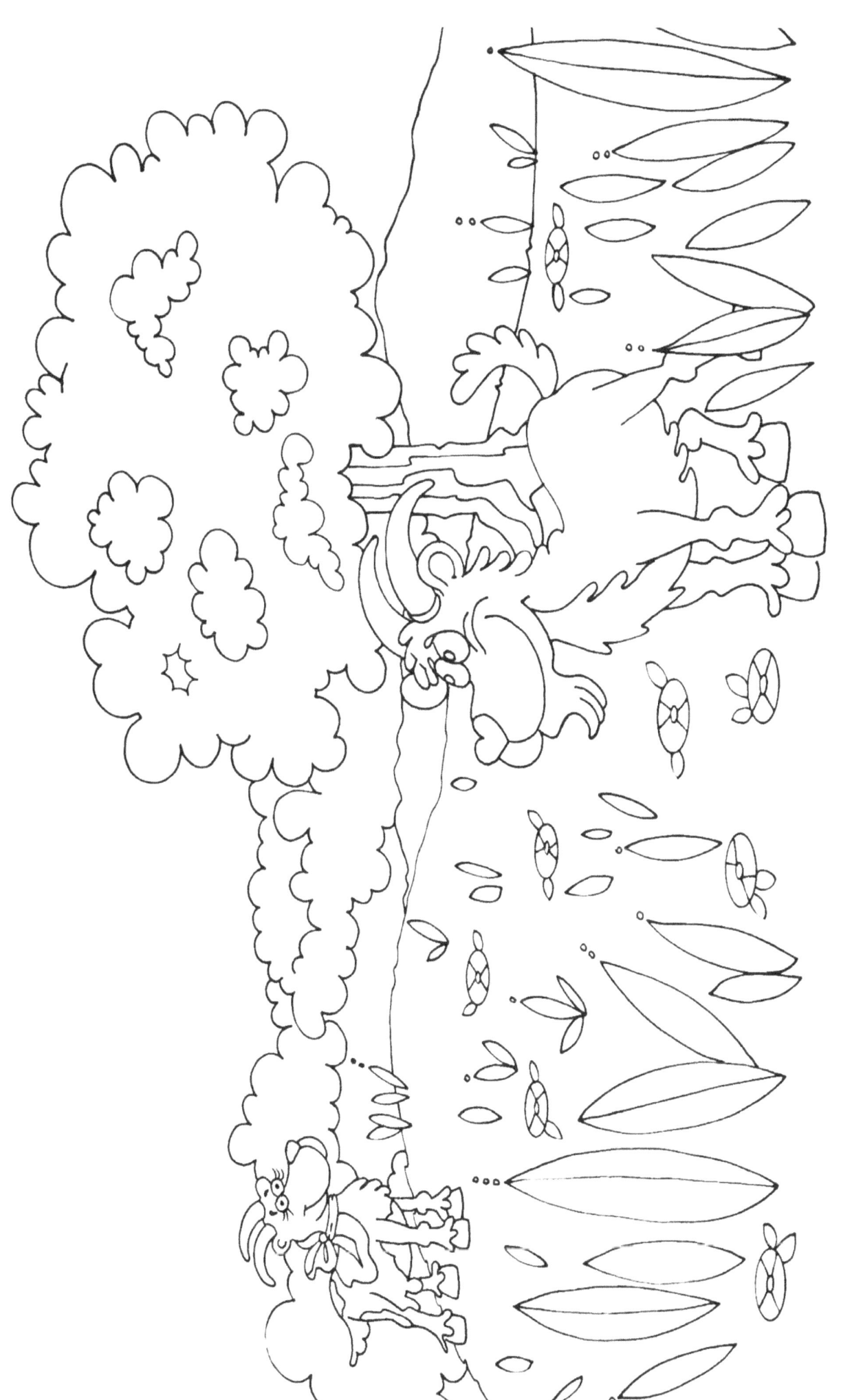

# G is for Goat — Goats can climb trees because they have excellent balance.

7

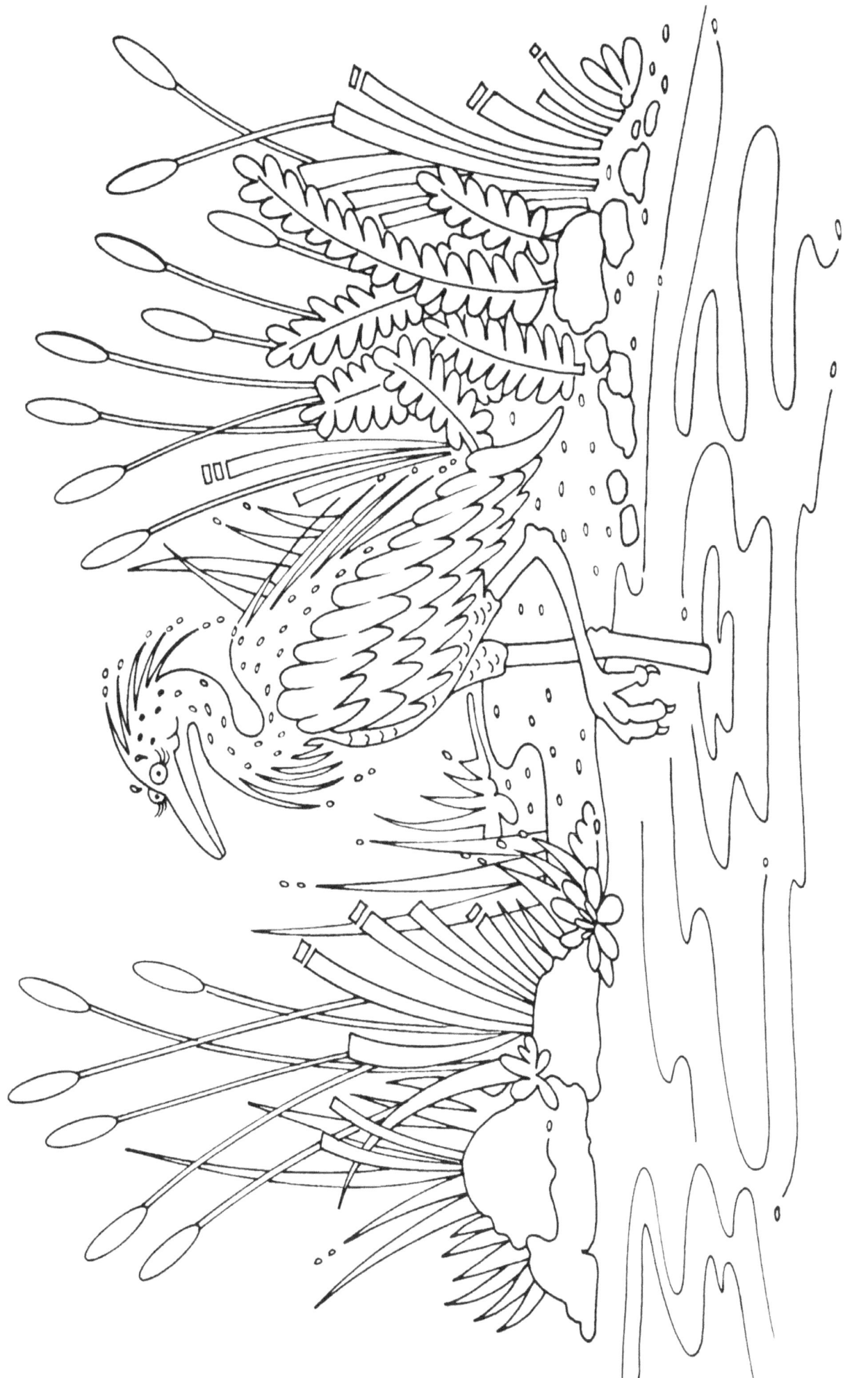

# H is for Heron – Herons stand motionless and wait for their food to come to them.

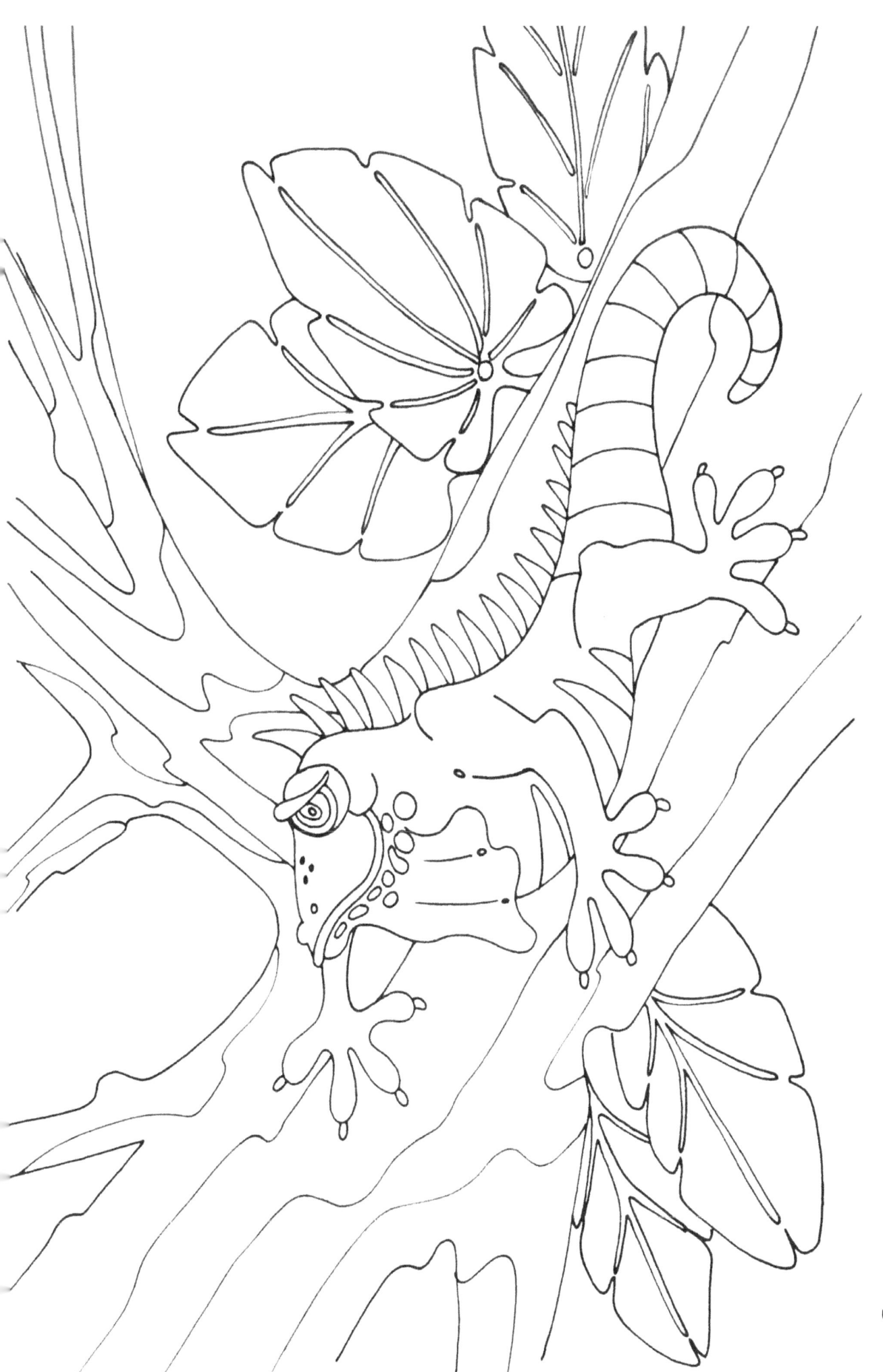

**I is for Iguana** – Iguanas are cold blooded and lay in the sun to warm their body.

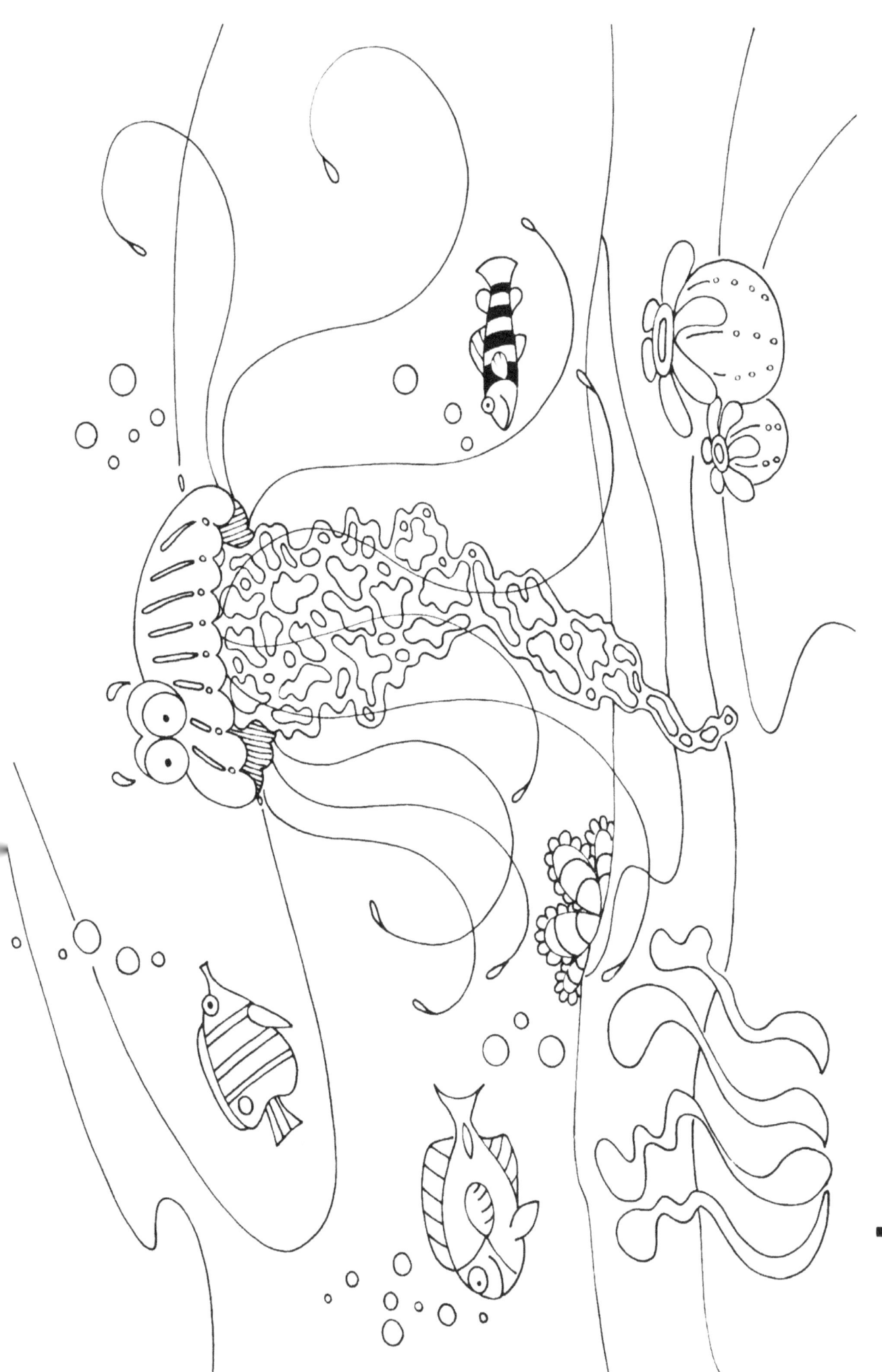

**J is for Jellyfish** – Jellyfish live in the ocean and does not have a brain.

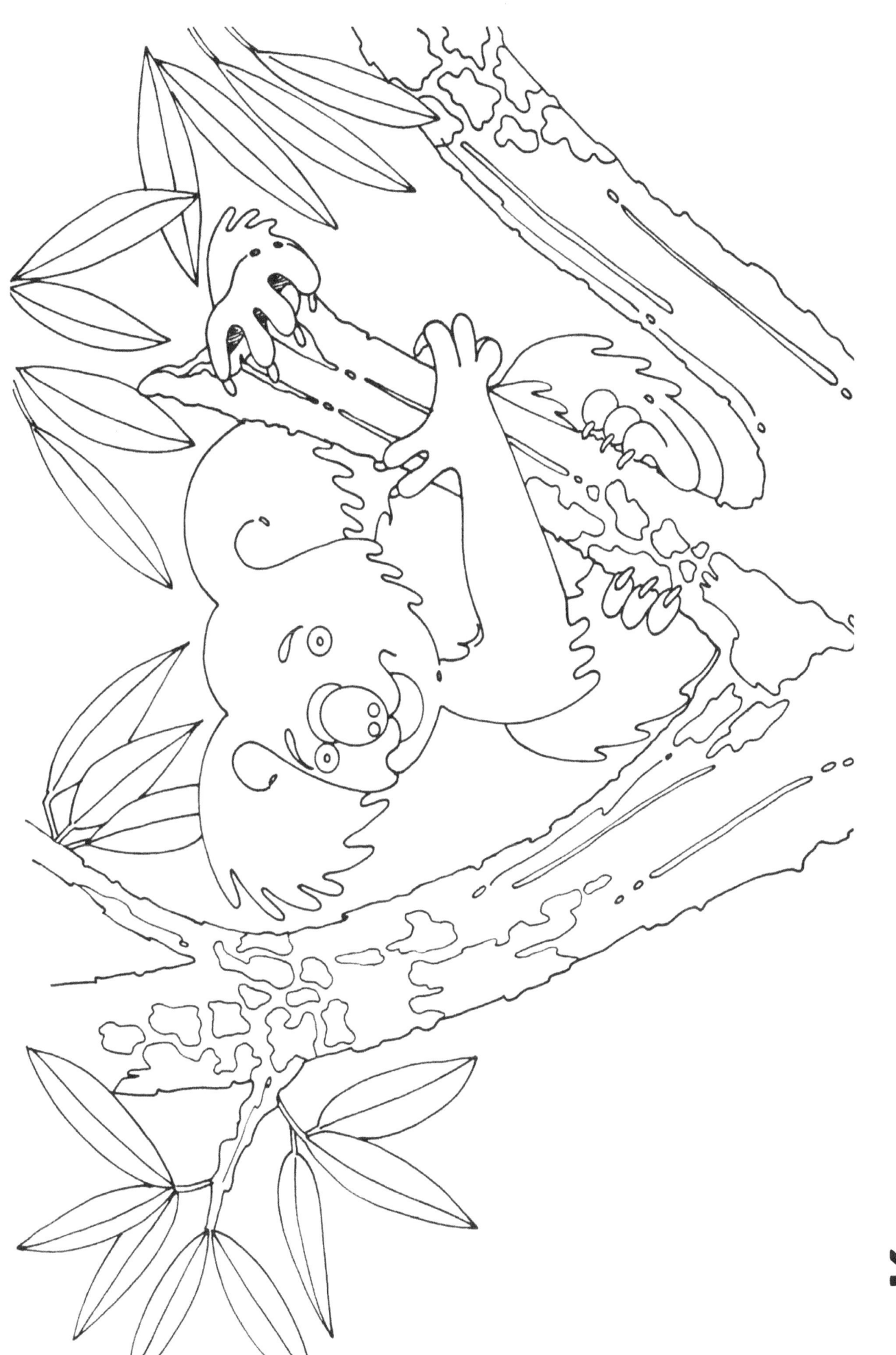

**K** is for Koala — Koalas eat eucalyptus leaves and sleep 20 hours per day.

11

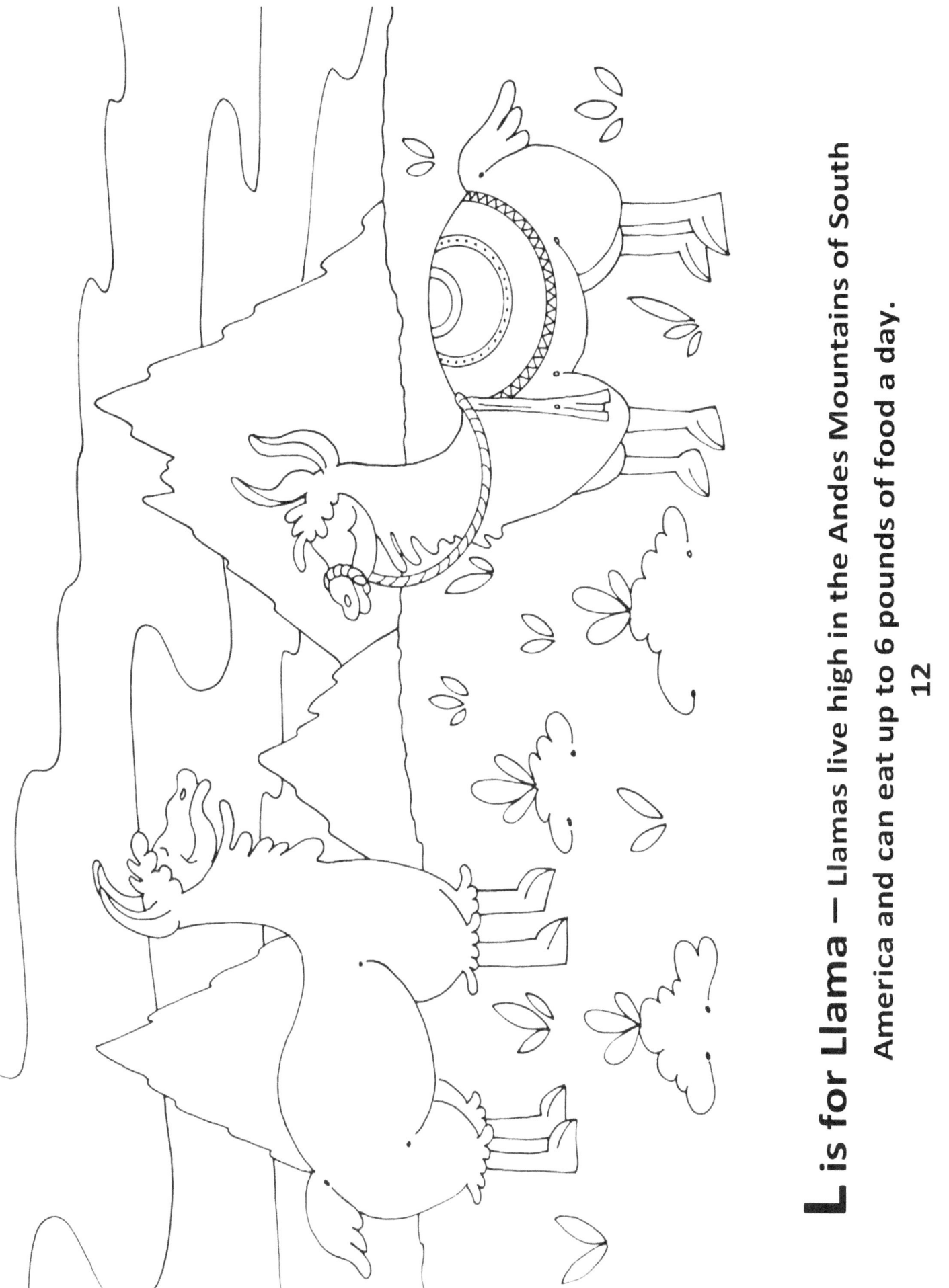

# L is for Llama — Llamas live high in the Andes Mountains of South America and can eat up to 6 pounds of food a day.

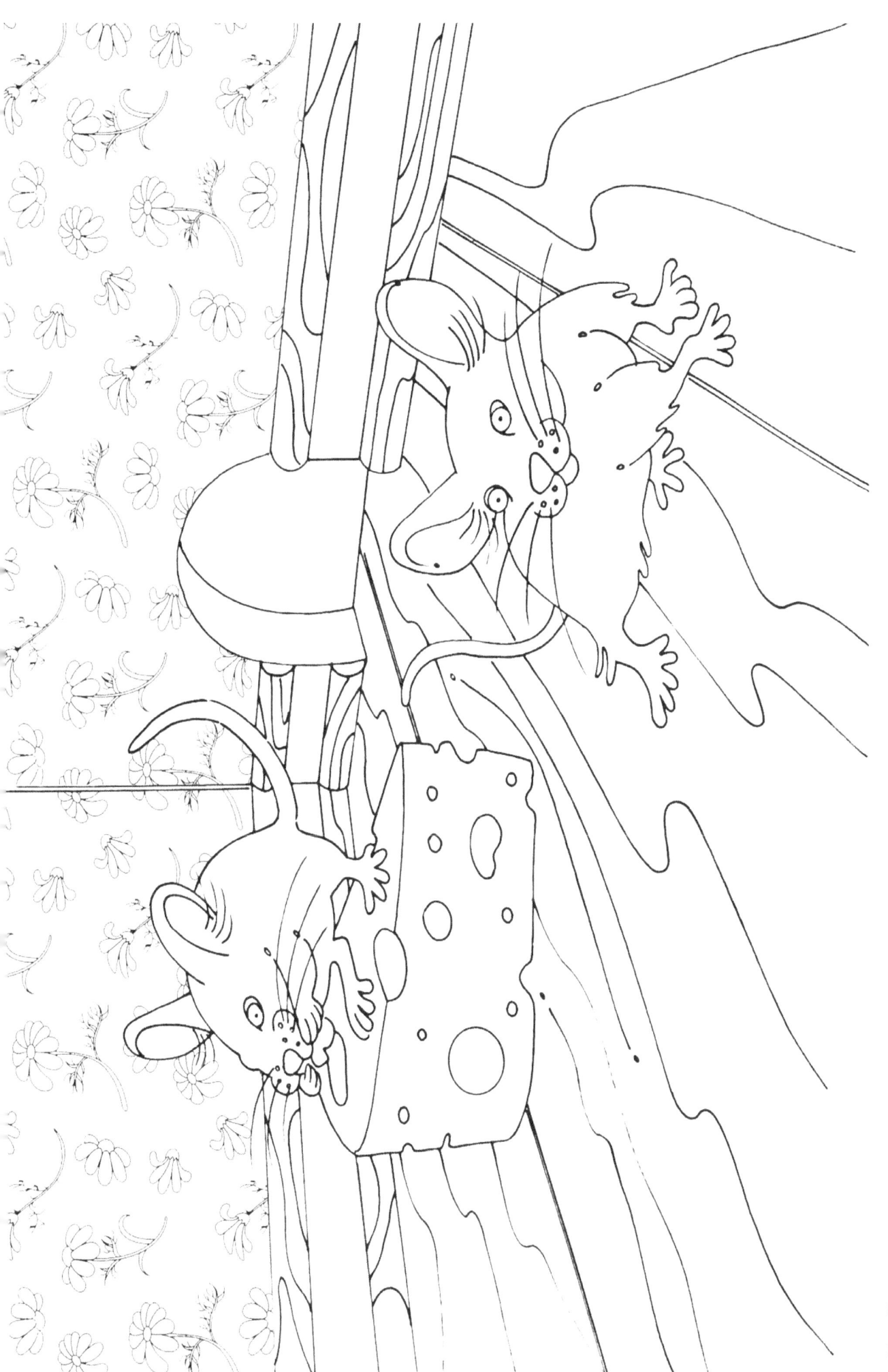

# M is for Mouse – A Mouse or plural Mice has poor eyesight but very very good hearing.

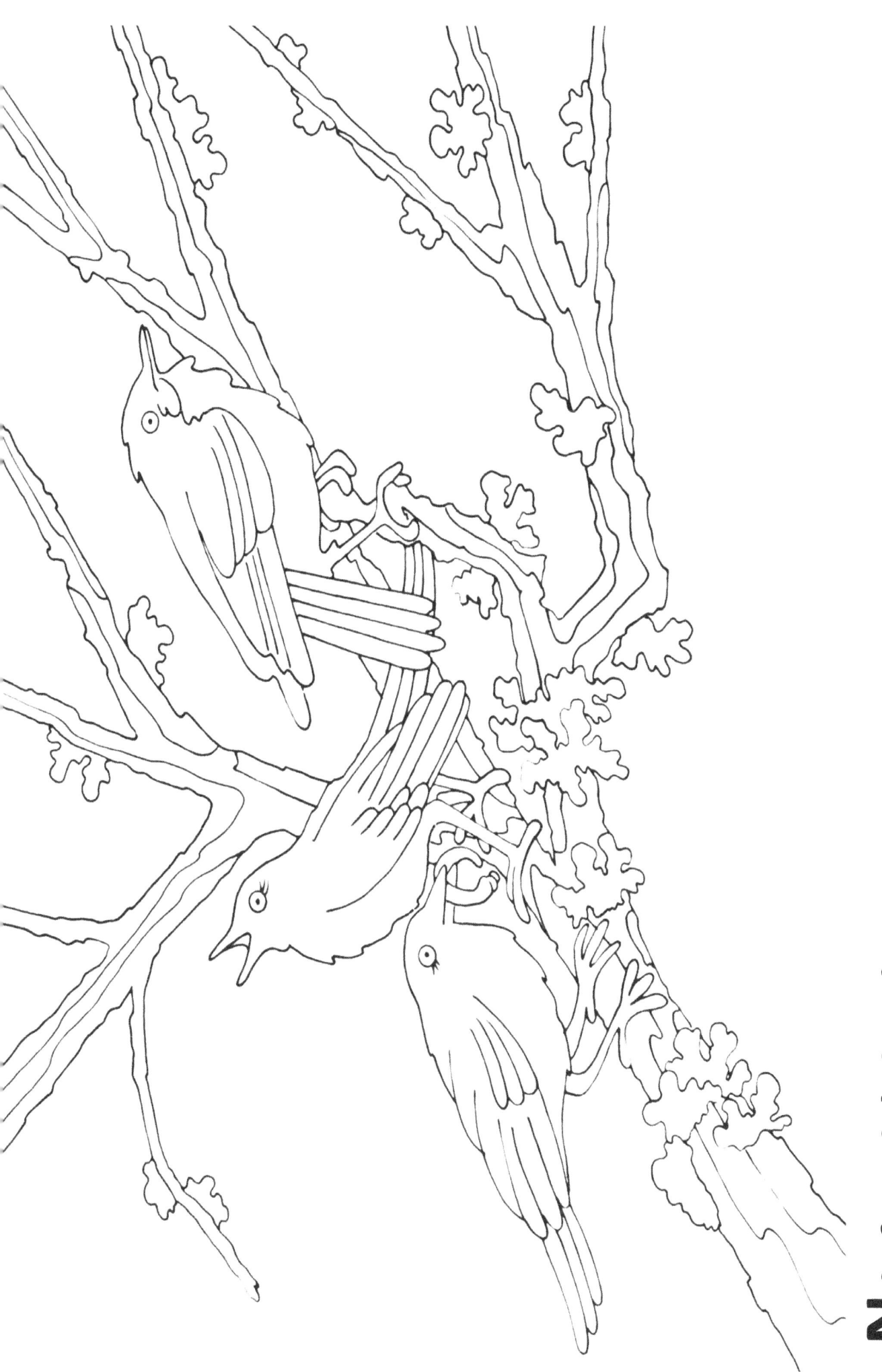

**N is for Nightingale** – The Nightingale are known for their beautiful singing voice.

14

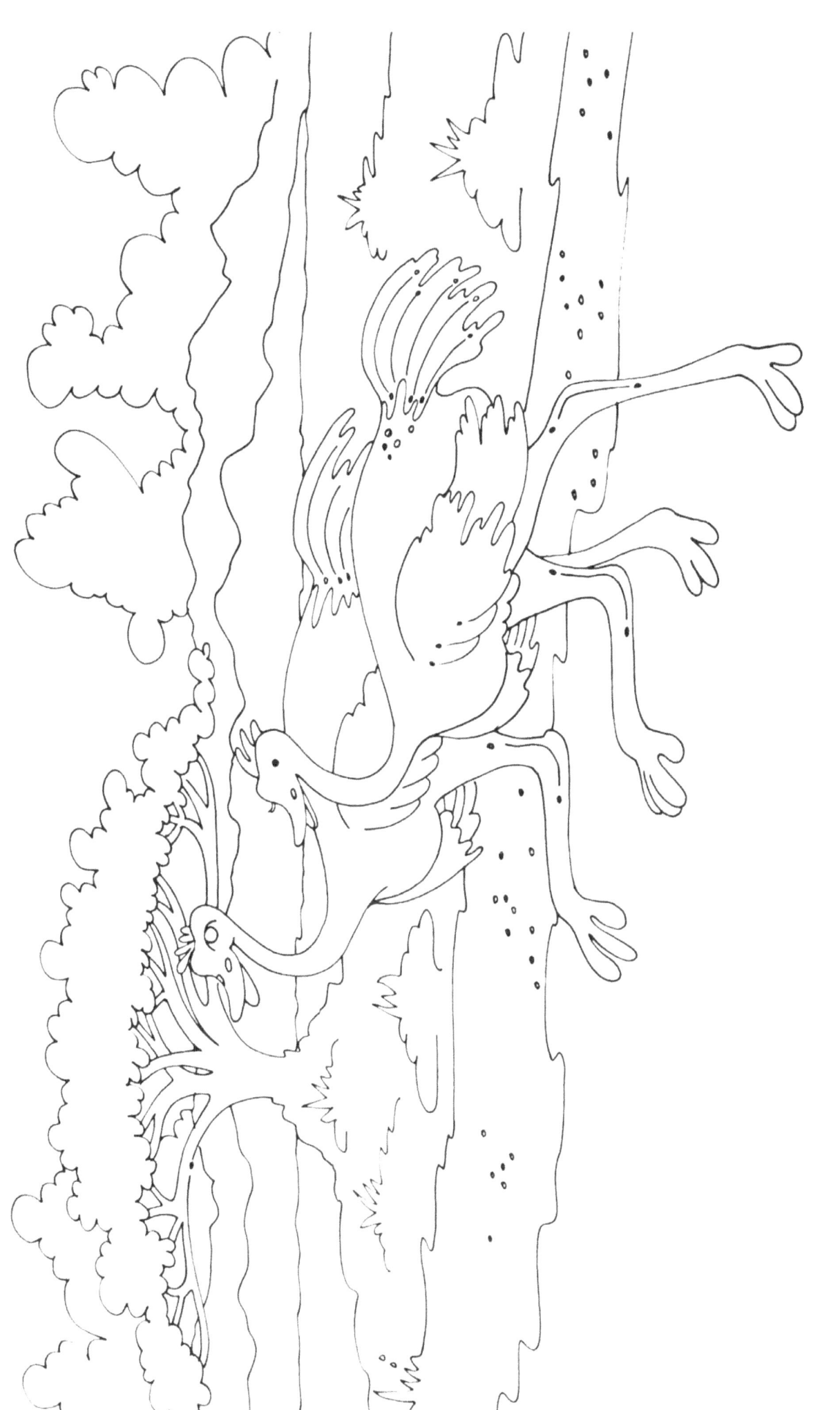

# O is for Ostrich – The Ostrich is the world's largest flightless bird.

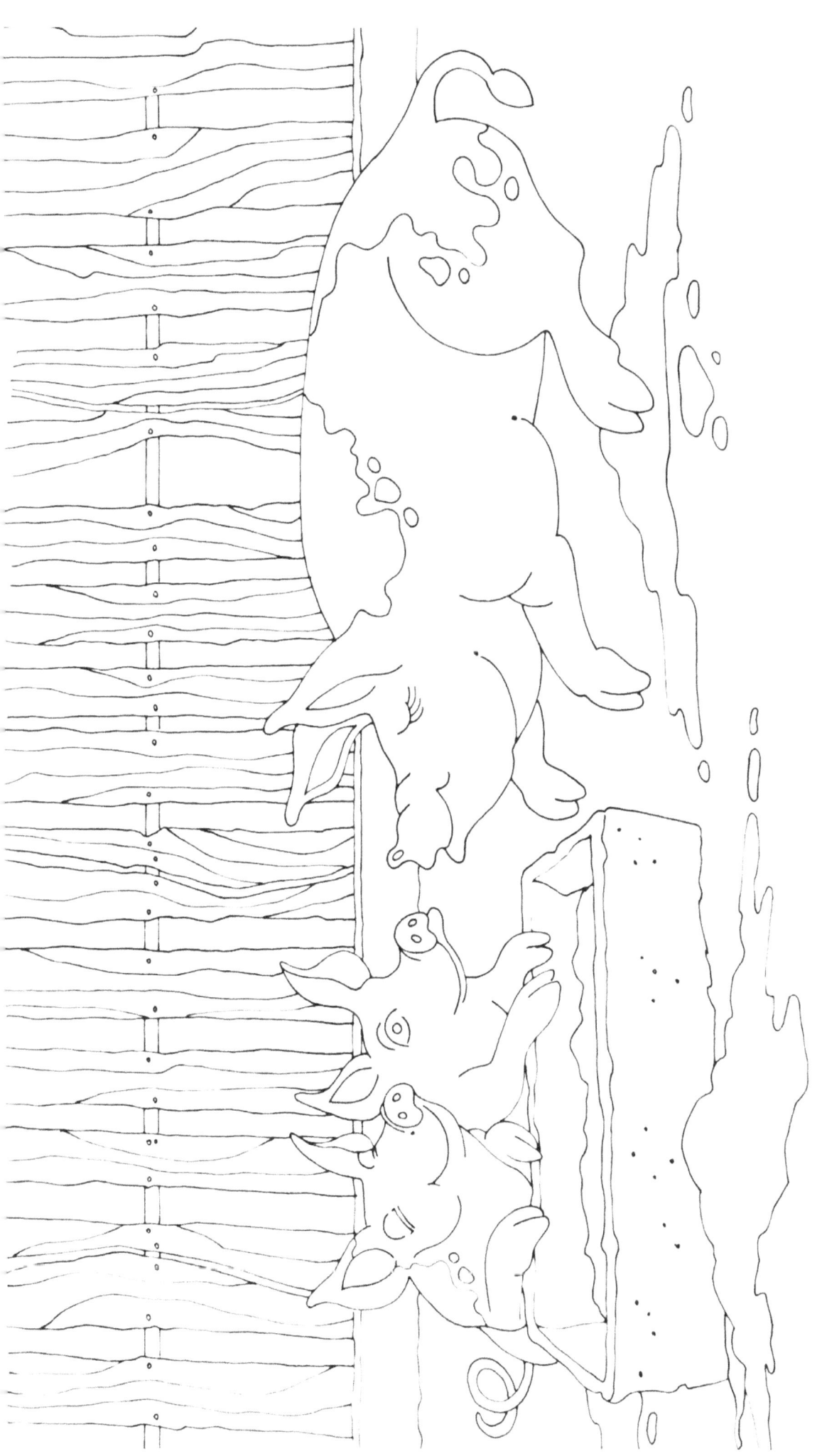

**P is for Pig** – Pigs are very smart and have a keen sense of smell.

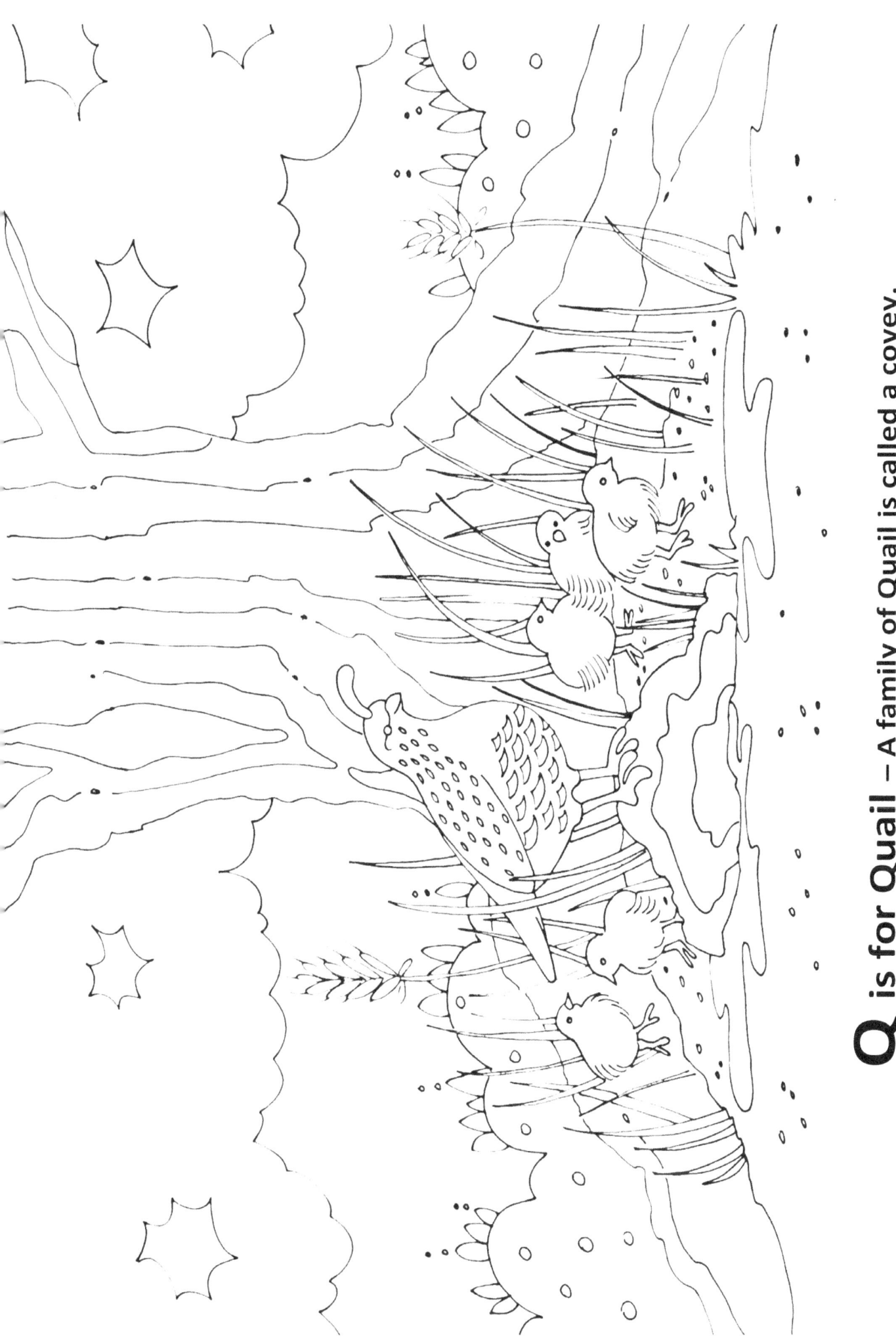

**Q is for Quail** – A family of Quail is called a covey.

17

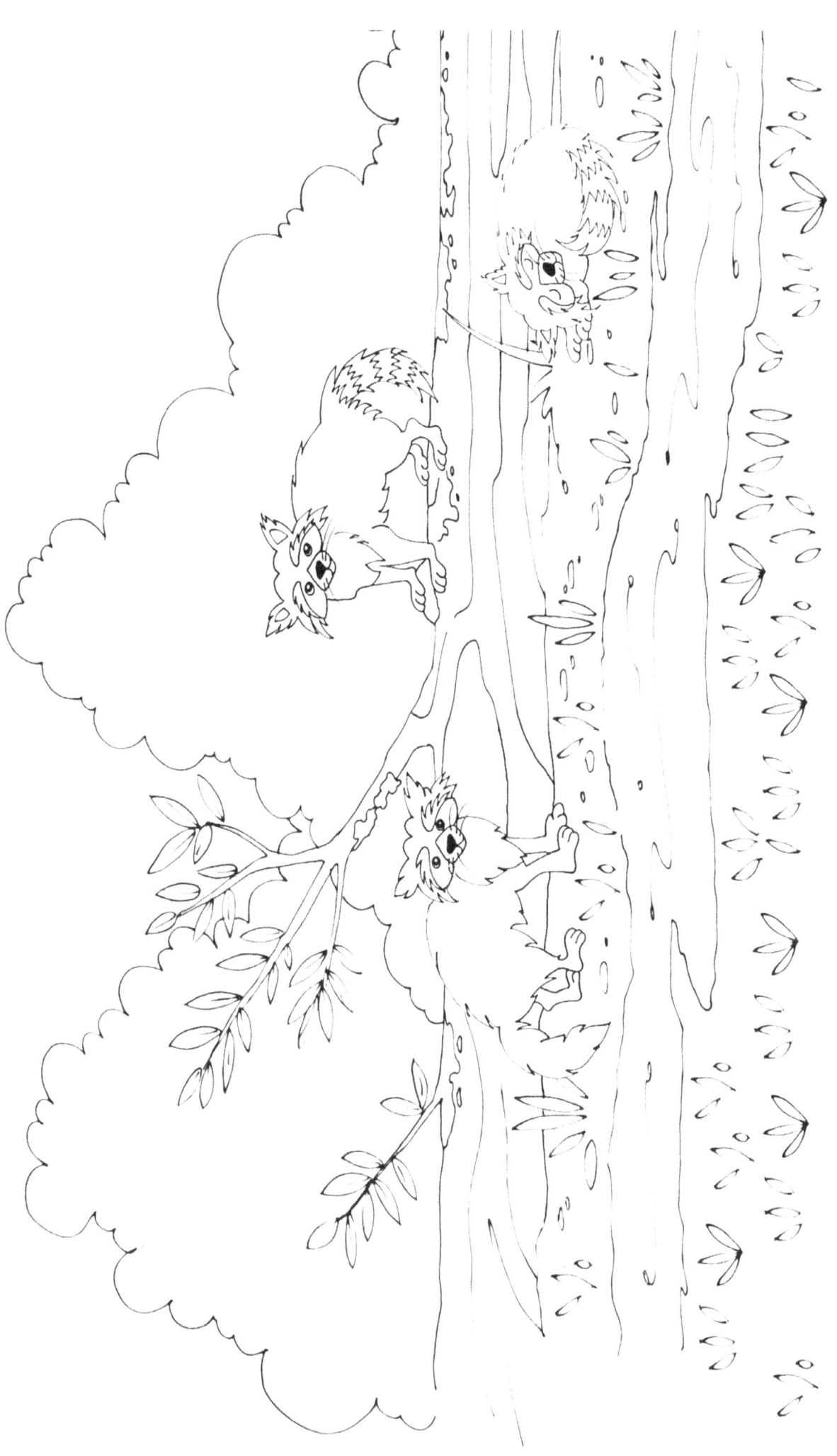

# R is for Raccoon
– Raccoons are nicknamed bandits due to their black mask and enjoy putting their food and hands in the water to wash.

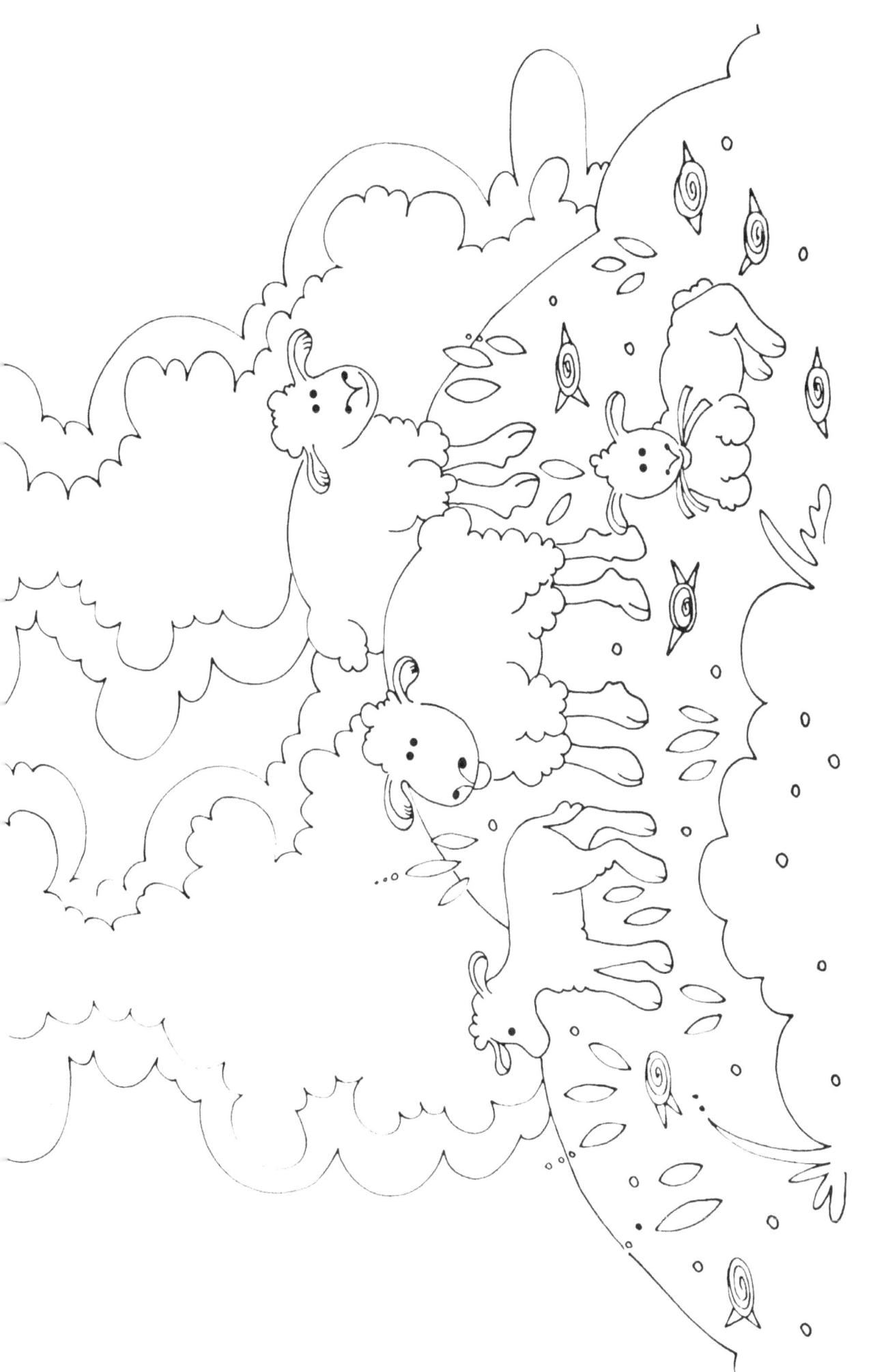

**S is for Sheep** – Sheep only have eight teeth and they are all on their lower jaw.

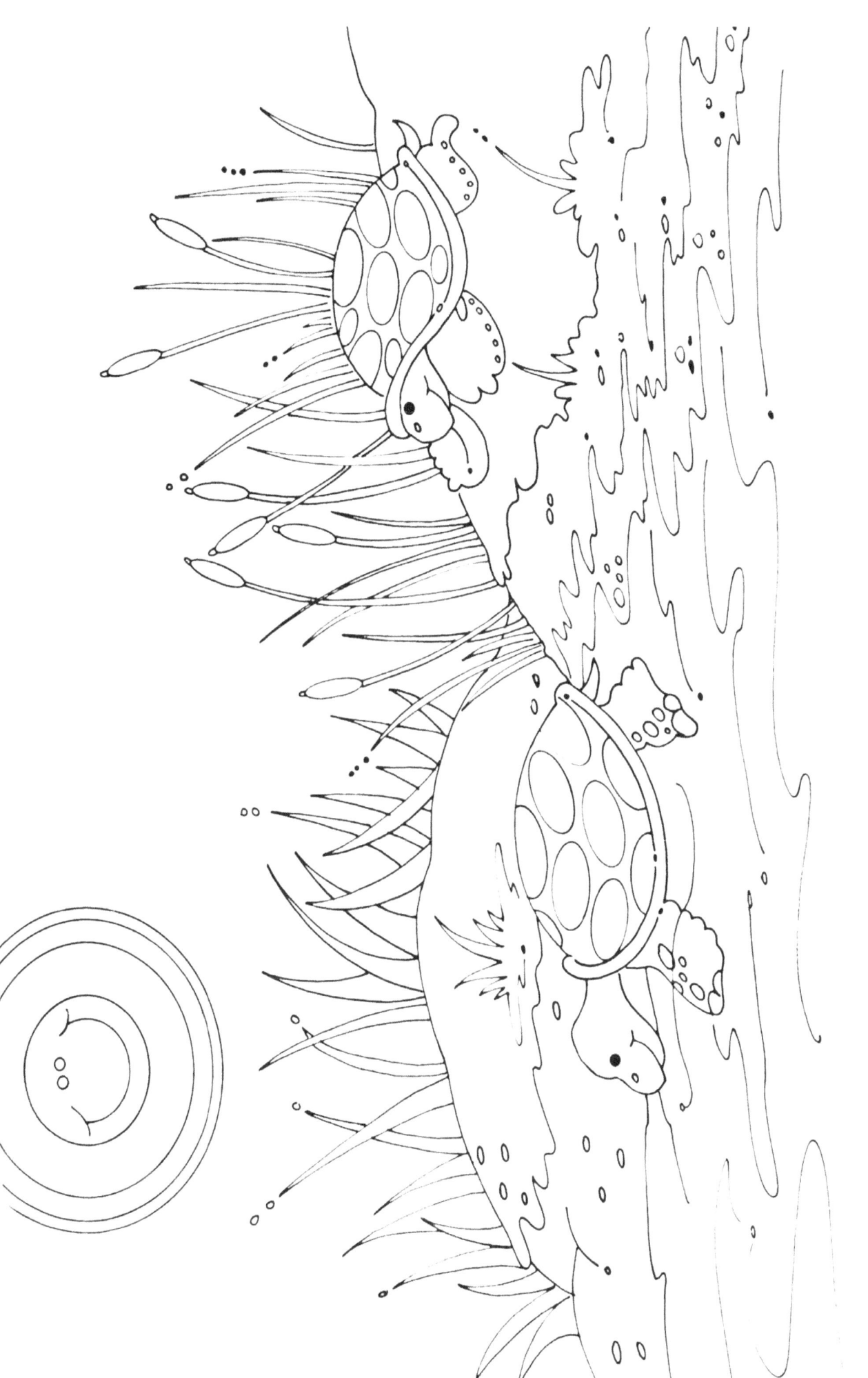

# T is for Turtle – Turtles have been alive for more than 200 million years.

20

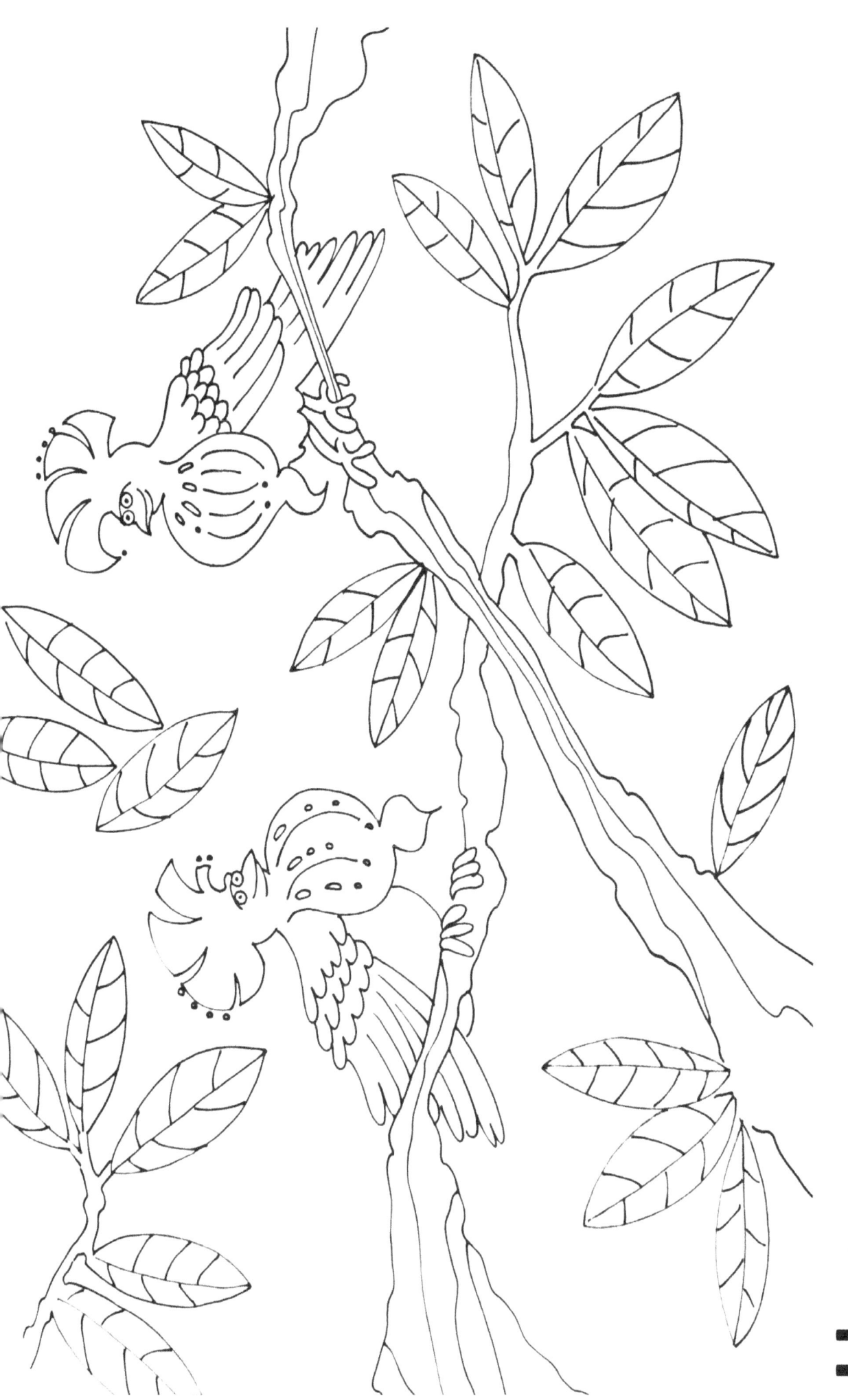

# U is for Umbrellabird

– Umbrellabirds have umbrella like head feathers. They fill their chest with air to make the loud booming calls they are known for.

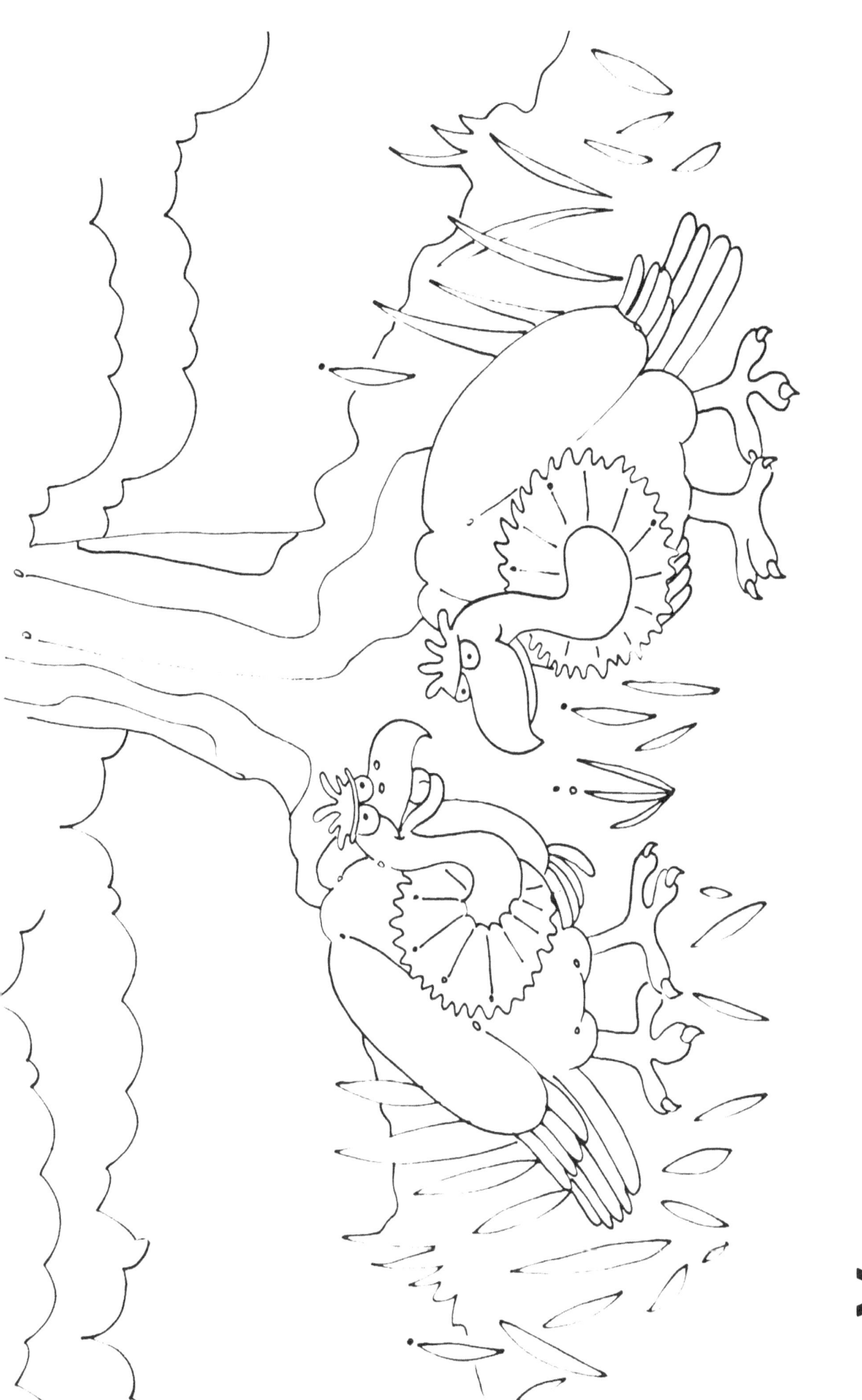

**V is for Vulture** – Vultures eat as much as they can at each meal and may find it difficult to fly with the added weight.

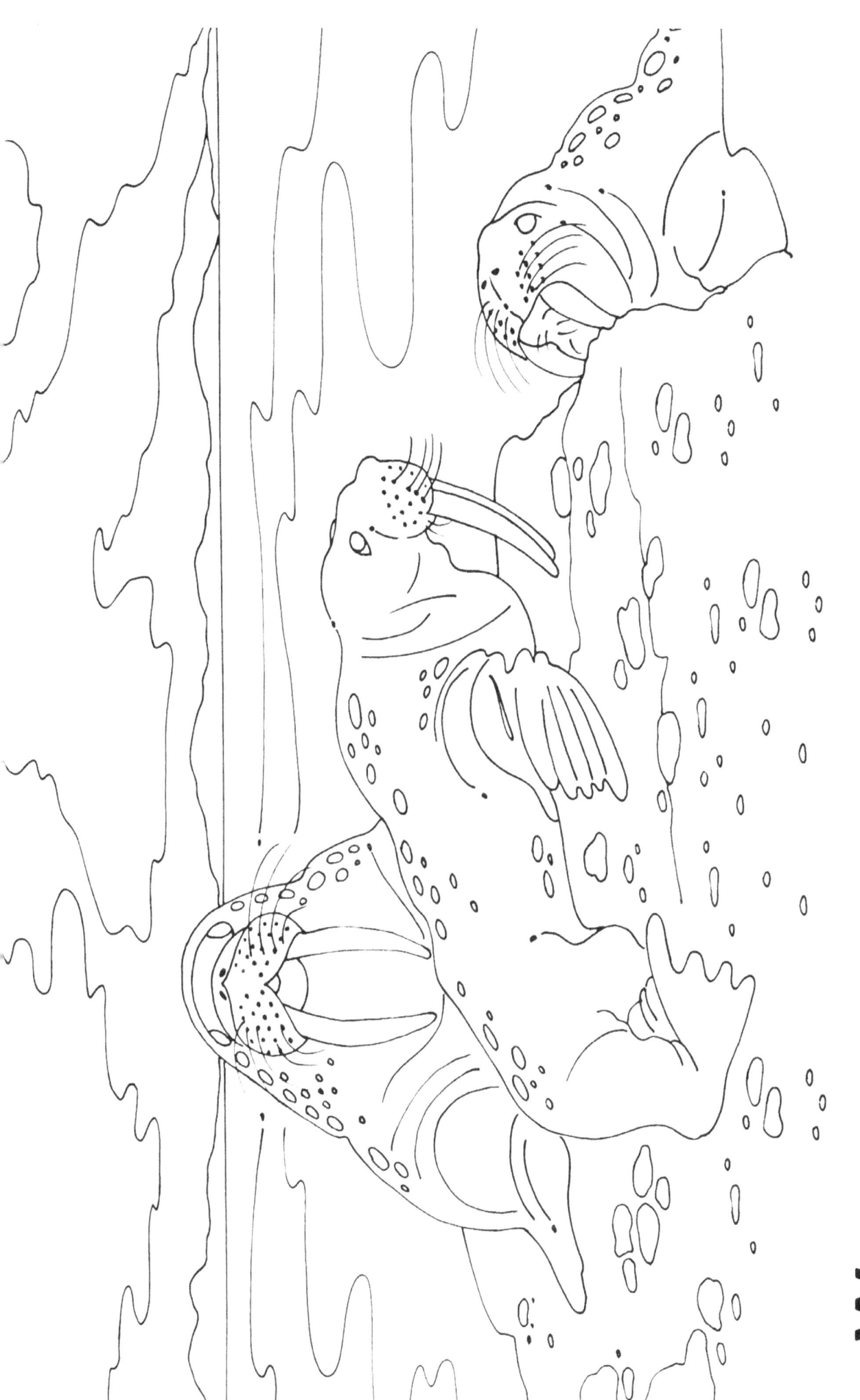

**W is for Walrus** – Walrus can hold their breath under water for up to 30 minutes while using their whiskers to find food at the bottom of the ocean.

23

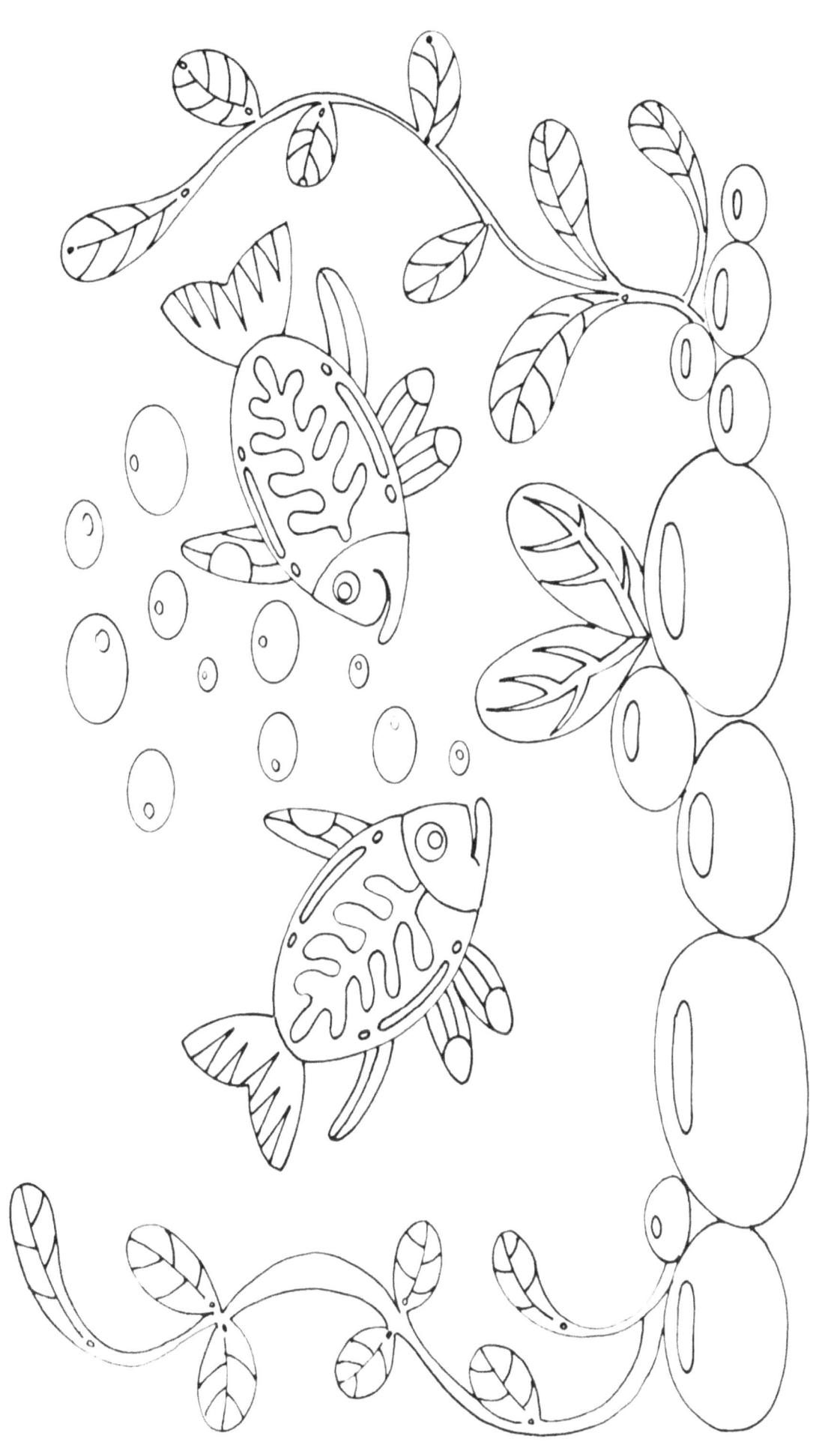

# X IS FOR X-Ray Tetra

X-Ray Tetra fish got their name because they have transparent skin that allows you to see their bones.

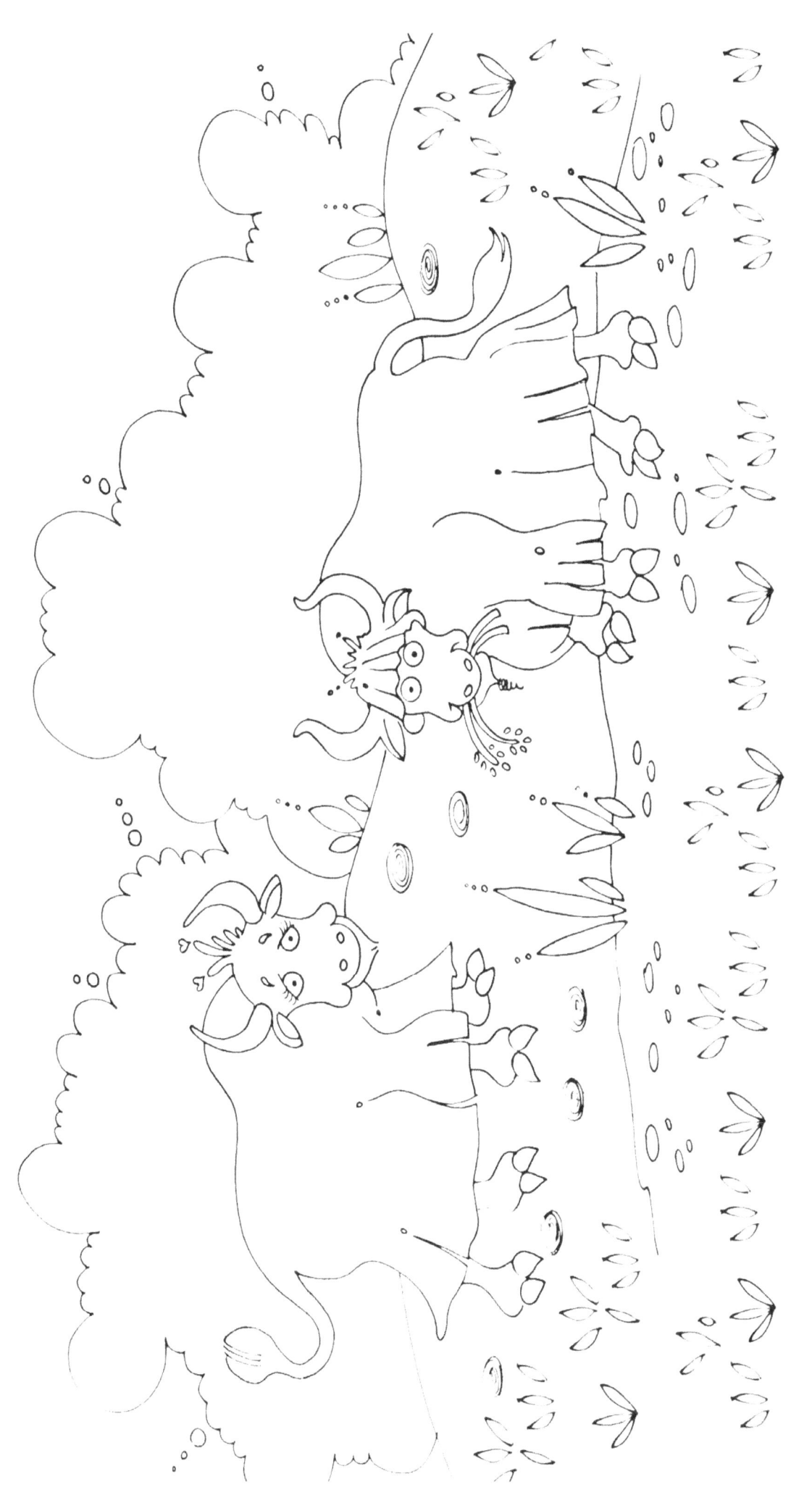

**Y is for Yak** – Yaks are the highest dwelling animal in the world living at 9,800 – 16,400 feet and can climb up to 20,000 feet above sea level.

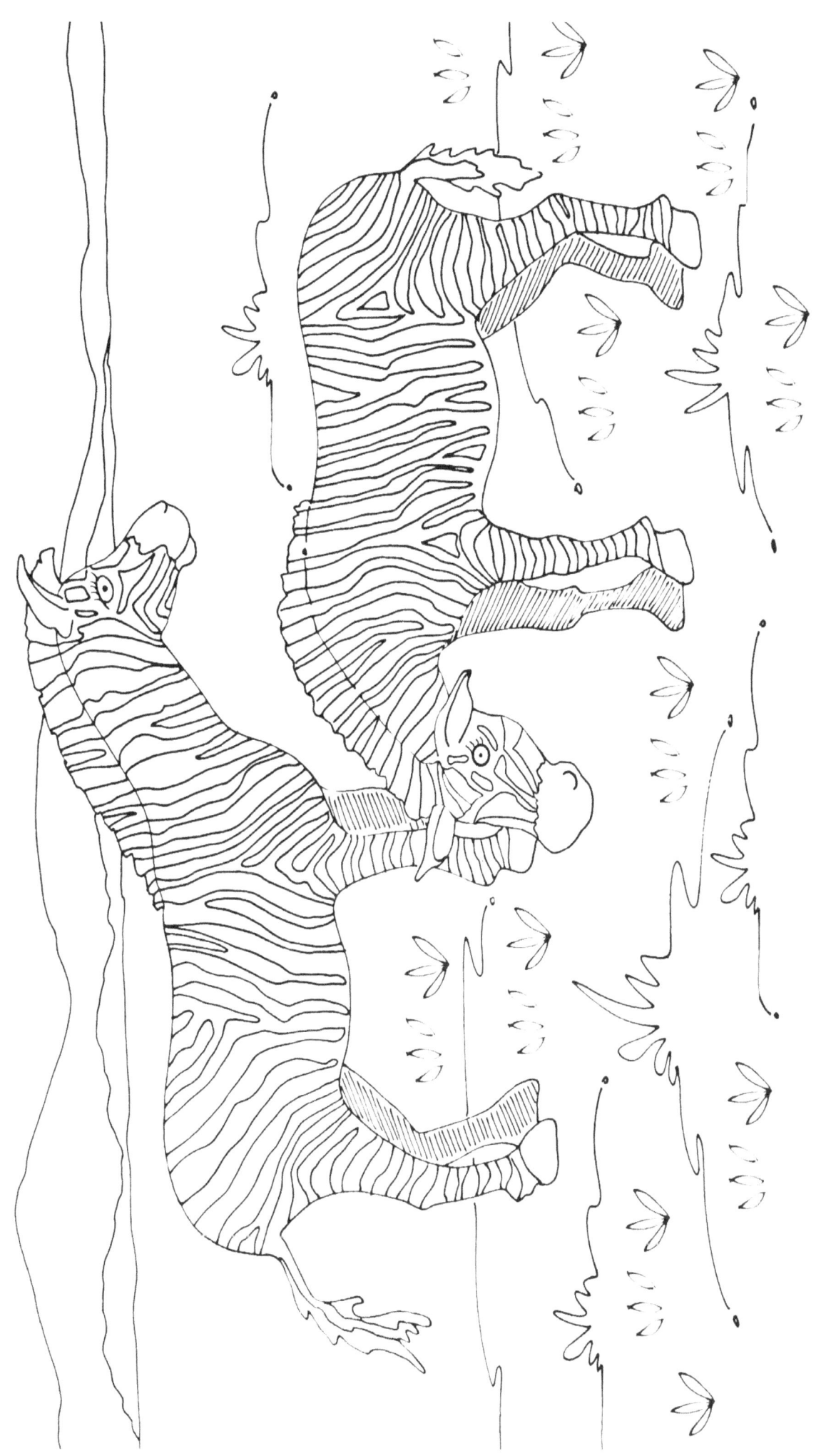

**Z is for Zebra** – Zebras are covered in black and white stripes and no two zebra stripes are alike. Zebras live in Africa and are related to the horse.

26

www.ingramcontent.com/pod-product-compliance
Lightning Source LLC
Chambersburg PA
CBHW062342220526
45469CB00008B/2803